QUESTIONS AND ANSWERS ABOUT WHAT ANIMALS EAT

by **RUTH BELOV GROSS** ■ illustrated by **MARSHALL PECK III**

SCHOLASTIC INC.

NEW YORK TORONTO LONDON AUCKLAND SYDNEY

CONTENTS

GIRAFFES

Giraffes live in Africa and in zoos all over the world.

A giraffe is a very tall animal. It has long legs and a long neck. A giraffe's mouth is a long way from the ground.

How tall is a giraffe? Think of three grown men standing one on top of the other. The man at the very top would probably be able to look a giraffe in the eye.

What do giraffes eat?

It isn't easy for a giraffe to bend its neck. So giraffes look for things they can eat when they are standing up straight. They like tree leaves best. They tear the leaves from the branches with their long, strong tongues and their long, thin lips.

In the zoo, giraffes get leafy branches as a special treat. They also get hay and oats, apples and bananas, carrots and potatoes, cabbage and bread. They get blocks of salt to lick too. Everything is put high up for the giraffes. Even water is put high up.

How do wild giraffes in Africa drink water?

A wild giraffe has a hard time when it is thirsty. It has to spread its legs wide apart. That is the only way it can get its head low enough to drink from a stream or water hole.

GIBBONS

Gibbons are members of the ape family. They live in the forests of southeast Asia, where they are very noisy. They are noisy in the zoo too. When you go there, you can hear them calling and singing and howling and whooping a long way off.

A gibbon has long arms. It uses them to swing through the trees. First it takes hold of a branch with one hand. Then it leaps and takes hold of another branch with the other hand. Sometimes it seems to be flying through the trees.

While it is moving from branch to branch, it grabs some food. Gibbons like fruit, leaves, and flowers best, but they eat insects and birds' eggs, too. Once in a while a gibbon will catch a young bird and eat it.

How does a gibbon drink water?

A gibbon has a special way of drinking water. When it finds a tree that is over the water, it holds on to a low branch with one hand and swings down to dip the other hand in the water.

Then it licks its hand and hairy arm.

Gibbons cannot swim. So they have to be very careful not to fall into the water when they are getting a drink.

ELEPHANTS

An elephant's trunk is really a long upper lip. It is also the elephant's nose. The elephant uses it for eating and drinking.

Watch an elephant pick up a bundle of hay with its trunk. The elephant wraps its trunk around the hay and stuffs it into its mouth.

When an elephant is thirsty, it sucks up water in its trunk and squirts it into its mouth.

How much food does an elephant eat?

An elephant eats a lot. Elephants that live in zoos eat about 300 pounds of hay every day. But that's not all. They eat oats. They eat whole loaves of bread. They eat buckets of cabbages, potatoes, carrots, apples, and oranges. And they drink about 50 gallons of water a day — 800 glasses!

What do wild elephants eat?

Wild elephants do not have things like bread and potatoes to eat. In Africa and India, where they live, elephants eat all the grass, leaves, roots, twigs, and fruit they can find. Mostly they eat grass. When they have eaten everything in sight, they move to a new place to look for more food.

It takes a lot of food to fill an elephant up, so wild elephants walk many miles a day looking for food.

BRONZE CUT WORM

BUTTERFLIES, MOTHS, AND CATERPILLARS

Butterflies and moths start out as tiny eggs. The eggs are usually laid on leaves.

Do you know what comes out of the eggs when they hatch? Take a guess.

If you said butterflies or moths, guess again. The answer is *caterpillars*.

SPHINX

What do caterpillars eat?

A caterpillar eats whatever it was born on.

Most caterpillars are born on the leaves of trees or plants — even on grass.

Some are born on cabbages.

Some are born inside of apples or pears or peaches.

Some are born on corn.

Some are born on your wool clothes.

There are many different kinds of caterpillars. Every caterpillar is born on the right thing for it to eat.

ORN EAR WORM

BLUE FRUIT WORM

FORESTER

HUMMINGBIRD MOTH

When do caterpillars eat?

They eat all the time.

There is nothing for a caterpillar to do but eat. It eats and eats. It grows so fat that its skin bursts. But underneath it has another skin, a little bigger than the first skin.

The caterpillar eats some more. Its skin bursts again. It eats some more. Its skin bursts again. It eats some more.

At last it has eaten enough. It is a much bigger caterpillar than when it began eating.

ISABELLA (WOOLLY BEAR)

When a caterpillar has eaten enough, what does it do?

It stops eating. Its skin splits for the last time. Now it is no longer a caterpillar. It is a *pupa*. It has already made a little sack for itself. Some sacks are silk cocoons. Some are hard and clear.

What does a pupa eat?

A pupa does not eat anything. It is simply resting. And while it is resting it is changing and growing. At last it breaks out of its sack.

When it comes out of its sack it is no longer a pupa. It is a butterfly or a moth.

It will be a butterfly if the caterpillar came from a butterfly's egg.

If the caterpillar came from a *moth's* egg, what will it be? It will be a moth.

ISABELLA

LLOWTAIL

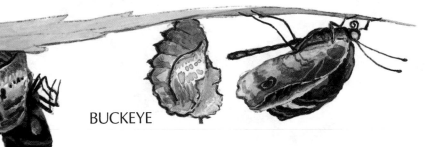

BUCKEYE

DAY MOTH

ADONIS BLUE

MEADOW FRITILLARY

What do butterflies and moths eat?

Some butterflies and moths do not eat or drink anything. They did all their eating when they were caterpillars. They ate enough to last for the rest of their lives.

Other butterflies and moths sip the sweet nectar of flowers. They also drink sweet, sticky tree sap and plant juices.

How does a butterfly drink?

It has a long tube attached to the front part of its head. The butterfly sucks nectar through this tube. When the tube is not being used, it is curled up underneath the butterfly's head.

Watch a butterfly land on a flower. *Whoosh!* Out comes the sucking tube.

Moths drink this way too.

GIANT ANTEATERS

The giant anteater's home is in South America, where it lives on ants and termites. When an anteater is grown, it is six or eight feet long — about as long as your living room sofa.

Giant anteaters have long sticky tongues, and they have sharp claws on their front feet. The sticky tongues and the sharp claws help them get their food.

They use the claws to break open the nests that ants and termites live in. These nests are as hard as cement. With their long sticky tongues they lick up the ants or termites inside.

An anteater can move its tongue very fast. It flicks it in and out of the nest. Each time the tongue comes out of the nest it is covered with hundreds of insects.

The giant anteater has no teeth, but it doesn't need teeth. Ants and termites are soft and don't have to be chewed.

What do giant anteaters eat in zoos?

Zoos can't give anteaters the same food they get at home. But the anteaters seem to like their zoo food anyhow.

In a zoo, anteaters usually get a creamy mixture of milk, eggs, chopped meat, baby cereal, and vitamins. They lick it up with their long tongues.

What do ants eat?

Ants will eat almost anything as long as it is juicy. They do not like food that is completely dry.

What do termites eat?

They eat wood mostly. In forests and jungles they eat rotten logs and fallen trees.

LIONS

At home in Africa, lions live together in groups. A group of lions is called a *pride* of lions. A middle-sized pride has one or two male lions, four or five female lions, and about a dozen lion cubs.

What do lions eat?

When they are hungry, lions eat any animal they can kill — a giraffe or a zebra, maybe, or an antelope or a buffalo. When lions are not hungry, they do not kill other animals. They hunt only when they need food.

Sometimes lions need food but cannot get any. They may not eat for a week when food is hard to find.

Do lions share their food?

In human families, parents make sure that the children have enough to eat.

Lions are different. They do not always share food with their cubs. On days when there is food, the male lions in the pride help themselves first. Then the female lions eat. The last ones to get any food are the lion cubs.

If there is not enough food, the lion cubs go hungry. Sometimes they die because there is not enough food.

But what would happen if the cubs ate all the food and the grown lions starved to death? Soon the cubs would starve to death too. Lion cubs are too young to hunt for their own food. But as long as the grown lions have enough to eat, they can always have more cubs later.

What do lions eat in the zoo?

Some zoos feed their lions chunks of raw meat. In other zoos, lions get meat, vitamins, and minerals, all mashed up together. It looks something like liverwurst.

BABY BIRDS

A baby songbird cannot see. It cannot fly. It cannot do much of anything. About the only thing it can do is eat.

As soon as baby songbirds hatch out of their shells, the parent birds begin to stuff them with worms and caterpillars and bugs. The baby birds eat everything their parents give them.

How much can a baby bird eat?

A man in England spent a whole day watching a nest of young robins. He counted the number of times the parent birds brought food to their babies.

The nest had five baby birds in it. The parents had to bring enough food for all five.

The parent birds hurried back and forth to the nest all day. Each time they came back they brought two or three caterpillars.

At the end of the day the parents had brought about 1,000 caterpillars home for their hungry babies.

How do birds feed their babies?

The parent birds bring food in their bills. Sometimes the mother bird and the father bird take turns going for food.

Sometimes the father bird brings the food back and puts it in the mother bird's mouth. Then the mother bird puts the food in the baby bird's mouth. She stuffs it far back into its throat.

How can the parents tell where to put the food?

When the parents land on the nest, the baby birds can feel the nest shaking. They get very excited. They stretch their necks and open their mouths wide.

The nest is often dark. But the inside of a baby bird's mouth is bright red or bright orange or bright yellow. The parents see these bright spots in the nest and poke food into them. Then they rush off to get more food.

EARTHWORMS

Earthworms live in the ground. It is cool and dark and damp there, just the way earthworms like it.

Earthworms move around in the ground even when the soil is hard. Can you guess how they get from one place to another?

They *eat* their way through! An earthworm just gobbles up the soil in front of its face. It makes a tunnel this way. The tunnel is called a *burrow*.

What do earthworms eat?

Earthworms eat bits of grass and leaves and other things that are in the soil. They get this food while they are making their tunnels under the ground.

On cloudy days and at night, earthworms come out of the ground to look for food. Each earthworm sticks its front end out of its burrow. It grabs a leaf or a blade of grass and pulls it down into the burrow.

Why do gardeners and farmers like earthworms?

The tunnels that earthworms make are like tiny pathways in the soil. These pathways help plants grow because they help bring air and water to the roots.

Earthworms help gardeners another way. Soil goes in an earthworm at one end and comes out the other end. When it comes out it is better soil than it was before. It is good fertilizer. Earthworms leave this good soil in little piles on the ground.

SEA LIONS

Some people make a mistake and say "trained seal" when they really mean "sea lion." The playful animals you see in the circus or at the zoo are probably California sea lions.

Sea lions can jump five feet out of the water and can be taught to do tricks. Maybe you have seen a sea lion balance a ball on its nose.

What food does a sea lion like best of all?

Sea lions like fish, fish, fish. They get fish as a reward when they learn to do a trick right.

Do sea lions like meat?

They won't touch it.

Can sea lions tell the difference between fish and meat?

They can tell every time. If you throw a fish into a pool full of sea lions, the sea lions rush to get the fish. But if you throw a piece of meat into the pool, the sea lions don't go near it.

They can tell the difference in the dark. They don't even have to swim over to find out.

TIGERS

Most tigers live in India. They are members of the cat family. Like most cats, tigers like to be alone. They live alone and hunt alone. Tiger cubs stay with their mothers until they learn to hunt by themselves. Then they are on their own.

A tiger usually hunts for food at night. Tigers have good eyesight and can see in the dark better than people can. During the day they take naps in the shade or lie in a water hole to keep cool.

What do tigers eat?

Tigers eat other animals. They like deer and wild pigs best, but they will eat any animal they can find — a baby elephant or a camel or a turtle. Sometimes tigers go to a nearby village and kill the cattle there.

On many nights tigers do not find anything at all to eat.

When a tiger kills an animal that is too big to eat all at once, it eats part of the animal and saves the rest. But a tiger can eat as much as 50 pounds of meat at one time. After a tiger eats, it drinks a lot of water.

Do tigers eat people?

Tigers will eat people only if they are very hungry and cannot get anything else to eat.

MOSQUITOES

What do mosquitoes eat?

Mosquitoes eat people. That's not exactly true, of course. Mosquitoes *bite* people. When a mosquito bites you, it sucks a little bit of your blood. That makes you itch. But the mosquito has had a good meal.

Only female mosquitoes can bite you. Male mosquitoes can't bite people. They can only sip plant juices and nectar.

Why do mosquitoes bite some people but not other people?

Some people just smell good to mosquitoes. Nobody knows just what kind of smell a mosquito goes for. But it is true that some people are hardly ever bitten by mosquitoes. Other people get lots of mosquito bites.

Scientists think it has nothing to do with the way a person's blood tastes to the mosquito. If it did, the mosquito would have to bite you first to see if you tasted good.

DRAGONFLIES

What do dragonflies eat?

Dragonflies eat mosquitoes. They also eat bees, butterflies, moths, and horseflies. But they like mosquitoes best.

You can see dragonflies near streams and ponds on a hot summer day. They dart and swoop and glide in the air. They are always on the lookout for something to eat.

How does a dragonfly catch its food?

A dragonfly catches its food in the air and eats it in the air. When a dragonfly sees something good to eat, it zooms over to get it.

Like all insects, dragonflies have six legs. The legs are all bunched up in front. The dragonfly makes a basket of its legs and scoops up the food in this basket. Then it uses its front legs to put the food in its mouth.

Do dragonflies eat a lot?

A dragonfly has a big appetite. A dragonfly can have more than 100 mosquitoes in its mouth at a time. One man saw a dragonfly that couldn't close its mouth because it was so full.

Another man wanted to see how much a dragonfly could eat. He caught a dragonfly and gave it 40 horseflies. The dragonfly ate all the horseflies in two hours and was ready for more.

BEARS

Black bears and brown bears are always ready to eat.

They like sweet things especially, but they will try anything. In the United States, bears used to get a lot of garbage from trash cans in the national parks.

Now most of the trash cans in the parks are bear-proof. Maybe the bears will stop looking for garbage. Maybe they will learn to get their own food in the mountains and forests.

What do bears find to eat in the mountains and forests?

Here are some of the things black bears and brown bears find to eat:

Fruits and berries
Nuts and seeds
Roots
Grass
Leaves

Flowers
Pinecones
Squirrels
Chipmunks
Mice
Fish
Ants

Honey from beehives
(When bears raid a beehive,
they will even eat the bees!)

What do zookeepers feed the bears?

In zoos, bears usually get meat, fish, and bread. They also get apples, carrots, celery, and other fruits and vegetables.

Bears are very greedy and will beg for food even when they have had enough.

BEES

What do honeybees eat?

Honeybees eat the honey they make. They make it for themselves. They eat some of it in the summer and save the rest for the winter.

In the summer, the bees gather nectar from the flowers. They mix it with bee saliva. They put it in wax cells in the beehive. Then they fan it with their wings to dry it out. That is how they make honey.

Bees eat pollen too. Pollen sticks to the bees' feet when they land on flowers. The bees carry the pollen back to the beehive on their feet.

Do bumblebees make honey?

They make just enough for themselves. Honey is their food too.

Bumblebees do not live through the winter the way honeybees do. So they do not have to save their food. They use it up in the summer.

COWS

Cows are big eaters. They have to eat a lot to make milk. Farmers know this, and they give their cows plenty of food.

What does a cow eat?

A cow eats grass, hay, grain, and corn. Every day she has about 60 pounds of food. You would have to eat about 200 plates of spaghetti to get that much food.

And every day a cow drinks about 20 gallons of water. That's 320 glasses of water.

To get all that food, do cows have to eat all day?

No. They do not spend the whole day eating. This is what they do:

Cows swallow their food fast. They do not even take the time to chew it first.

The food goes straight to a special place in the

HOLSTEIN

cow's stomach. This place is called the *paunch*. It holds a lot of food.

Food stays in the paunch for several hours, getting nice and soft.

Later on, when the cow is resting, the food comes back to her mouth. It comes back in small balls. It is easy to chew. The cow grinds up each ball of food with her teeth. Then she swallows it for good.

Each ball of food is called a *bolus*. This is what a cow chews when we say she is chewing her cud. Animals that chew cuds are called *ruminants*.

Cows usually chew their cuds lying down. They look very content.

JERSEY

CAMELS

Camels are animals with humps on their backs. Some camels have one hump. Other camels have two humps. All camels are ruminants. (See page 41.)

Camels with one hump are called dromedary camels. Most of them live in the hot, dry deserts of North Africa. Camels with two humps are called Bactrian camels, and they live in colder places. Some of them live in China.

Camels smell bad (but not to other camels). They spit and have nasty tempers too.

Do camels keep water in their humps?

No. They have fat in their humps. You can tell when camels get enough to eat by looking at their humps. Well-fed camels have plump humps. When camels do not get enough to eat, their humps sag.

BACTRIAN

What do camels eat?

Camels eat rough, tough plants and grasses. They are not fussy about their food. In zoos, camels eat hay. They get vitamins and minerals there too.

Can camels go without water?

If they have to, camels can go without water for two weeks or more. But it is better for a camel if it has water every few days.

When a camel has not had any water for a long time, it can drink a lot of water in a hurry. One thirsty camel drank more than 100 quarts of water in ten minutes. That's almost a bathtub full of water.

DROMEDARY

RACCOONS

Raccoons usually live in the woods. During the day they like to curl up in a hollow tree and go to sleep. At night they wake up and look for something to eat.

What do raccoons eat?

Raccoons eat almost anything. And they find their food almost everywhere.

They visit vegetable patches.

They raid cornfields.

They take eggs and small birds from their nests.

They fish for crayfish and trout.

They hunt for frogs and insects.

They eat fruits and nuts.

They go looking in garbage pails.

They even open refrigerator doors if they get the chance.

Do raccoons wash their food?

Raccoons often dip their food in water before they eat it. They slosh the food around in the water with their paws. That makes some people think that raccoons wash their food.

Scientists do not think that raccoons dip their food in water to wash it. They think the raccoons do it for some other reason.

Some scientists think that raccoons do it because wet food is easier for a raccoon to swallow.

Some scientists think that raccoons do it because they learned to feel around in streams and ponds for crayfish and other things to eat.

Some scientists think that raccoons do it just for fun.

KOALAS

What do koalas eat?

A koala has exactly one thing on its menu. It eats the leaves of eucalyptus trees. It can't eat *anything* else. If it does, it gets sick and dies.

Eucalyptus trees grow in Australia. And that is where koalas live.

Another name for eucalyptus tree is gum tree. The oils from its leaves are used in cough drops.

Koalas look like teddy bears. Some people call them koala bears. But koalas are not bears at all. And they do not smell like bears. They smell like strong cough drops. The koalas get that way from eating eucalyptus leaves.

In the United States there are only a few zoos where you can see koalas. The zoos are in California, and they grow eucalyptus trees especially for their koalas.

PORCUPINES

What do porcupines like best?

To a porcupine, anything salty is delicious. Sometimes a porcupine eats deer antlers that are lying in the woods. It eats the antlers because they have salt in them.

Perspiration is salty too — and people leave a tiny bit of salty perspiration on everything they touch. Porcupines are very good at finding these salty things, even after the perspiration is all dried up.

When a porcupine lives near a farmhouse or a cabin in the woods it has lots of tidbits to choose from. A porcupine has a feast when it finds

a salty, sweaty pair of shoes

a salty, sweaty ax handle

a salty, sweaty canoe paddle

a salty, sweaty toilet seat.

A porcupine has no trouble chewing any of these things because porcupines have four big front teeth.

What else does a porcupine eat?

In the spring and summer, a porcupine eats flowers and leaves. It eats tender green twigs. It eats fruits and vegetables too, if it can get them. Porcupines do not eat other animals.

In the winter, porcupines eat the bark of trees. This is very bad for the trees. One porcupine can kill many trees in its lifetime.

SNAKES

A snake eats only when it feels like it. That is not very often. Some snakes eat once a week. Some eat about every two weeks. Some snakes do not eat that often.

How do snakes eat?

Snakes do not chew their food. They always swallow it whole.

Then do snakes have to eat very small things?

No. Snakes can eat things that are much bigger than they are. They do it by opening their mouths very wide.

One kind of African snake can swallow a whole egg without breaking it. The egg is three or four times as big as the snake's neck. After the snake gets the egg down, it spits out the shell.

STARFISH

Starfish are not fish at all. But they do live in the sea. You can sometimes see starfish on the beach. They are left there by the tide.

Most starfish have five arms. Some starfish have more, though. If you cut a starfish in half and throw it back in the water, each half will grow into a whole starfish.

A starfish does not have teeth, and it does not have jaws. But it can still eat. Mostly it eats clams and oysters.

How does a starfish eat a clam?

A clam has two hard shells. They are tightly closed. So the first thing a starfish has to do is open the clam.

The starfish sits on top of the clam and holds on to the shells with its arms. Then it pulls hard. There are little suckers (called *tube feet*) on a starfish's arms.

The suckers help the starfish pull. The starfish keeps pulling on the shells until the clam gets tired and opens up.

Now the starfish is ready to eat. It turns its stomach inside out and pushes it out through its mouth. The mouth is in the middle of the starfish, on the bottom side.

Then the starfish slides its stomach between the shells of the clam. It wraps its stomach around the soft part of the clam. Juices from the starfish's stomach help to digest the clam.

That is the way a starfish eats a clam. When it has finished, the stomach goes back again into the starfish. It brings bits of clam back too. It goes back the way it came, through the starfish's mouth.

What do frogs eat?

A frog will eat just about any animal that will fit in its mouth.

Small frogs eat insects and worms mostly. Big frogs eat bigger things. A bullfrog is a big frog — about eight inches long. It eats small turtles, snakes, mice, and birds. It even eats other frogs.

A frog has a long sticky tongue. It is attached to the front of the frog's mouth. That way a frog can poke its tongue out farther than people can. (*Your* tongue is fastened to the back of your mouth.)

When a frog sees an insect it whips out its tongue to catch it. *Zip!* The insect is caught. It can't get away because it is stuck to the frog's sticky tongue.

BLUE WHALES

The largest animal in the world is the blue whale. It is bigger than a house. It is heavy too — heavier than any dinosaur that ever lived, heavier than many elephants all put together. A blue whale can weigh as much as 150 tons.

What does a blue whale eat?

It eats tiny animals that live in the sea. These animals are called *krill*. A krill looks something like a shrimp. It is about as big as your thumb.

Why does such a big animal eat such small animals?

A blue whale has no teeth. So it cannot chew anything.

It has a very small throat. So it cannot swallow anything big.

Many other kinds of whales do have teeth and can eat big things.

Does a blue whale get enough to eat?

It certainly does. It can eat three tons of krill at a time.

When a blue whale is ready for a meal, it swims toward a spot that is full of krill. It opens its mouth. *Slosh!* The whale's huge mouth is full of water and krill.

Then the whale closes its mouth. But it doesn't swallow. The whale doesn't want to drink all that water. It just wants the krill. So it squirts the water out through special strainers in its mouth. The strainers are like big combs. They keep the food from going out with the water.

When the water is gone, the whale swallows the krill. Then it opens its mouth and does the same thing all over again. The whale does this again and again, until it has had its three-ton meal.

DINOSAURS

What do dinosaurs eat?

Dinosaurs don't eat anything. They aren't living anymore. They lived many millions of years ago, long before there were people.

When dinosaurs were living, they ate some of the same kinds of things that animals eat now.

Some dinosaurs ate plants that grew in the water.

Some dinosaurs ate plants that grew on land.

Some dinosaurs ate birds.

Some dinosaurs ate the eggs of birds.

Some dinosaurs ate insects.

Some dinosaurs ate other animals.

Maybe some dinosaurs ate fruit.

But there was one thing that some dinosaurs ate that no animal can eat today — they ate other dinosaurs.

PEOPLE

People are animals too. They are human animals. They eat many of the same things that other animals eat.

What do children eat?

Children eat all kinds of things. When they are very small, they drink lots of milk. Later, when they are older, they still drink milk but they eat other things too.

What do you like to eat? Milk? Fruit? Vegetables? Meat? Bread? Cereal? Boys and girls grow fast and stay healthy when they eat these things. Everybody needs to eat them every day.

Most boys and girls — and grown-ups too — also like to eat desserts and sweet things. They give you energy, and they are good for you if you don't eat too much of them.

What do children like best?

This is what some eight-year-old American girls and boys said they liked best:

Spaghetti	Watermelon
Tootsie Rolls	Hamburgers
Ice cream	Chicken
Pizza	Hot dogs
Jelly	

What food do *you* like best?

for Willy

Acknowledgments

The author wishes to thank the many specialists who reviewed sections of this book — staff members of The American Museum of Natural History, The New York Zoological Society, The Central Park Zoo/Wildlife Conservation Center, and the Cooperative Extension Association of Suffolk County, New York.

ISBN 0-590-48449-4

12 11 10 9 8 7 6 5 4 3 2 1   6 7 8 9/9 0 1/0
Printed in the U.S.A.   08

First Scholastic printing, October 1996

Book design by Laurie Williams